Good Dog!
Dog Care for Kids

By Beth Adelman

The
Child's World®
www.childsworld.com

Published in the United States of America by The Child's World®
P.O. Box 326 • Chanhassen, MN 55317-0326
800-599-READ • www.childsworld.com

Thanks, Carol.—Beth

ACKNOWLEDGMENTS

The Child's World®: Mary Berendes, Publishing Director

Produced by Shoreline Publishing Group LLC
President / Editorial Director: James Buckley, Jr.
Designer: Tom Carling, carlingdesign.com
Cover Art: Slimfilms
Copy Editor: Beth Adelman

Photo Credits
Cover—Photos.com (4).
Interior—All photos by Bonnie Nance/Rural Image,
except the following: 7, 14, 23 (Dreamstime.com).

LIBRARY OF CONGRESS CATALOGING-IN-PUBLICATION DATA

Adelman, Beth.
  Good dog! : dog care for kids / by Beth Adelman.
      p. cm. — (Girls rock!)
  Includes bibliographical references and index.
  ISBN 1-59296-743-4 (library bound : alk. paper)
  1. Dogs—Juvenile literature. I. Title. II. Series.
  SF426.5A34 2006
  636.7—dc22
                                   2006001653

CONTENTS

WHAT YOUR Dog needs

Your dog is always there for you. She plays with you when you're happy and cuddles with you when you're sad. She listens to all your secrets and never tells. With all she gives you, there are a few things you need to give her.

The number one thing your dog needs is a **routine**. Dogs like to know when things are going to happen.

Your dog needs to eat and go for walks and play several times a day. She'll be happier if those all happen at about the same times every day.

Dogs look forward to the time they spend with you.

A cool **canine** collar is a must for every dog. There are lots of colors and styles to choose from. You can pick one that makes your dog look like a fashion queen (or king). Nylon collars come in bright colors and patterns, and leather collars may have fancy designs.

Doggy To-Do List

Make a list or a chart of all the things your dog needs every day and when they should be done. Decide with your family who will be in charge of each job. Then everyone will know what they are supposed to do and when. That way, your dog will know she can count on all of you.

A must-have accessory for your dog's collar is a tag that identifies her. It should have your dog's name and your family's phone number.

Your dog's collar shouldn't be too tight or too loose—just snug enough that you can fit two fingers between the collar and her neck. A puppy may need different collars as she grows.

Dogs love to eat, and most of them will eat just about anything. That's why it's up to you to make sure your dog eats the good stuff. That means top-quality dog food and healthy snacks.

Dogs love snacks, but make sure you feed them healthy snacks.

Dogs are **carnivores**, which means they eat meat. Read the label on the dog-food bag or can, and make sure there's plenty of meat in your dog's food. More meat is better for your dog.

Your dog doesn't need to eat chocolate or raisins, even though you might think they're tasty. Both foods can make her really sick.

Meat, carrot pieces, green beans, apple slices, and small bites of cheese make good doggy snacks.

Use a special doggy shampoo to keep your dog's coat beautiful.

Not door mats—mats here mean tightly packed clumps of hair.

Whether she has long hair or short hair, straight or curly, your dog needs regular **grooming**. This helps keep her coat healthy and free from tangles and **mats**. She may also need a bath.

It can be fun for both of you to brush and comb your dog regularly. Start when she's a puppy and she'll grow to love it. Be patient and gentle, and be extra careful around her head, feet, and tail.

Parting the hair means dividing it to make a line, just like the one on the girl in this picture.

When you're grooming your dog, **part** the hair and look all the way down to her skin for fleas or ticks. If you see any, tell your parents, because these little bugs can make your dog very itchy.

Brushing and combing your dog's hair is fun, and it's good for her, too!

It's very important to make sure your dog stays healthy. Just as you sometimes see your doctor, your dog should see the **veterinarian**, or "vet" (a type of doctor just for animals), at least once a year for a check-up.

Pronounce this word like this: veh-teh-ruh-NAYR-ee-un.

The vet may give your dog a shot to keep her from getting sick. The vet will check your dog's skin for fleas and ticks and look at her teeth. The vet will also look in your dog's eyes and ears, and feel her all over to see if she has any lumps and bumps.

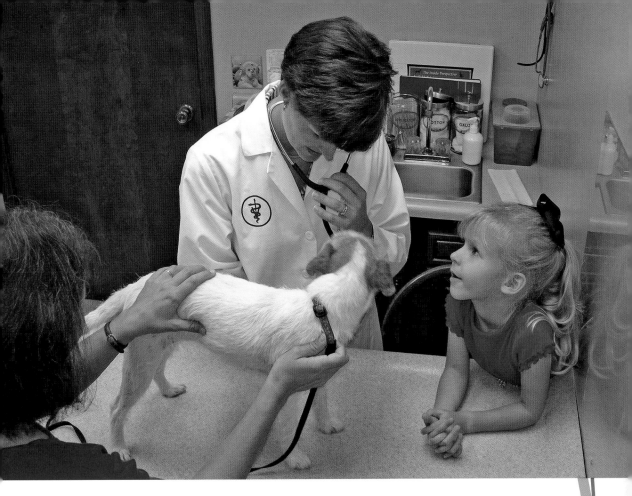

If your dog suddenly stops eating or doesn't want to play, or if she starts to limp or cry or just seems really different, she needs to go to the veterinarian right away. She's counting on you, remember!

When you go to the vet, it's a good time to ask questions about your dog's care.

Hey, where did everybody go? Dogs usually like to be around people.

With all the things dogs need, what don't they need? Dogs don't need to be left alone in the backyard. It can

get very hot or very cold out there, and anyway, they want to spend their time with you!

Your dog doesn't need to be bothered when she's eating or sleeping. She doesn't need you to touch her ears or eyes or mouth, or to pull or tug on her hair. (Giving her hugs is fine, of course!)

She doesn't need to be teased or hit or yelled at. Of course, you would never do those things to your dog. But it's up to you to make sure your friends don't, either.

How well do dogs smell? The average dog has more than 200 million scent receptors in its nose, compared with about 5 million for humans.

2

HOW TO
Speak Dog

You talk with your mouth, but dogs "talk" with their bodies. They use their ears and tails and even their hair to send messages to one another—and to you.

A calm dog will relax her tail and let it hang down. As she gets more excited, her tail will go higher. A curious dog will push her ears forward. A scared dog will pull her ears back.

When your dog lowers her front end and raises her back, she's saying "Play with me!"

OPPOSITE PAGE
Ears up, eyes on the prize, this dog is ready to learn a trick!

Be the Lead Dog

If your dog doesn't know who the leader is in your family, she'll put herself in charge. And then she could become bossy and not follow the rules you have set. Training your dog helps her understand that people are her leaders.

When you train your dog, you make a set of rules that help her live happily with you. She'll understand clearly what she should do and what she should not do.

When she's not sure, she'll look to you to be her guide. And that will make her feel very safe and confident.

Training helps you become closer with your dog, too!

You can use hand signals to help your dog learn what you want her to do.

Dogs are no different from us when it comes to learning. If you tell them they did something right and offer them lots of praise and pats for doing it, they'll do it again.

If you tell them they did something wrong and ignore them or walk away, they won't do it again. They like the pats and praise.

It's not easy for dogs to learn English, so you'll have to be patient. Praise your dog when she does the right thing.

Pick a phrase such as "uh-oh" to let her know when she's doing something wrong (like chewing the furniture). Dogs are smart, and they will learn almost everything you teach them.

It's fun to teach your dog tricks, and she'll enjoy learning new things. You can teach her to give you a kiss when you ask for one. All you have to do is wait until your dog licks your face.

Every time she does it, say, "Kiss. Good girl!" Keep doing this and she'll learn that the word "kiss" means "Please lick my face."

Make sure you tell her what a good girl she is every time she does it.

If your dog is not a kisser, you can encourage her to lick your face by putting something tasty on your cheek. Be patient and she'll soon learn to kiss you!

When you're hugging your dog, don't squeeze too tight!

3

TIME TO Play!

Most dogs play well with others. They like to play with kids, adults, other dogs, and even cats! If you leave them alone, dogs will play on their own a little bit, but mostly they will just sleep and feel bored.

For dogs, playing games with people is a lot more interesting. Your dog wants to play with you!

You can throw a ball or play chase or wave a flag. You can make things fly, roll, and bounce in interesting ways. Dogs like to play with things that move. Playing with you is so much better than playing alone!

Your dog needs regular playtime with you. A tired dog is a happy dog.

Many dogs love to play **fetch**, and there are lots of ways you can play this game. When you are teaching your dog to fetch, make it easy at first so she can learn.

It's true—dogs really do like to fetch sticks. They like chewing on them, too.

Here are some fun fetch games:

- **Bounce fetch:** Throw a bouncy ball down on a hard surface and let your dog catch the ball as it goes up.

- **Hide-and-seek fetch:** Throw your dog's toy as far as you can, and then hide. When she comes back with it, call her name and make her find you.

- **Soccer fetch:** Gently kick a big ball along the ground toward your dog and encourage her to chase it.

Little dogs like little toys, and big dogs like big toys. You can make dog toys yourself out of things you have around the house.

For little dogs, stick a treat inside an empty toilet paper roll and let your dog work at pulling it out. A plastic lid makes a nice mini-flying-disk.

For big dogs, cut off an old sock and stuff some of it back into the toe. Tie a knot in the top to keep the stuffing inside and you've got a fun chew-and-chase toy.

There is something special about having a dog for a friend. But remember that it's your job to help take care of your dog, too.

Make time for her, and she'll love you forever!

Having a dog takes time and work, but their love and kisses make it all worthwhile.

GLOSSARY

accessory   something you wear with something else to make it look better, such as jewelry or a hair clip

canine   another word for dog, or anything that is about dogs

carnivores   animals that eat meat

fetch   to get something and carry it back

grooming   to take care of the hair by washing, brushing, and combing

mats   hairs that get tangled up and form big clumps that have to be cut out

part   in this case, a line between sections of a hairstyle

routine   doing things the same way at the same time every day

scent receptors   tiny cells inside the nose that recognize various smells

veterinarian   a doctor who takes care of animals and is often called a "vet"

FIND OUT MORE

BOOKS

Dog Training for Kids
by Carol Lea Benjamin
(Howell Book House, Hoboken, NJ), 1988
Learn how to teach dogs basic obedience skills and even some
fun tricks.

Eyewitness: Dog
by Juliet Clutton-Brock
(Dorling Kindersley, New York), 2004
Discover the history and behavior of dogs and all their
cousins — wolves, jackals, and foxes.

Puppy Training for Kids
by Sarah Whitehead
(Barron's Educational Series, New York), 2001
Easy-to-understand instructions on puppy training and care.

Totally Fun Things to Do With Your Dog
by Maxine Rock
(John Wiley & Sons, Hoboken, NJ), 1998
Games and activities for kids and canines.

WEB SITES

Visit our home page for lots of links about dogs and dog care:
www.childsworld.com/links

Note to Parents, Teachers, and Librarians: We routinely check our Web links to
make sure they're safe, active sites — so encourage your readers to check them out!

INDEX

BETH ADELMAN is a Certified Animal Behavior Consultant and the former editor-in-chief of *Cats* magazine and *DogWorld*. She has won several awards from the Cat Writers Association and the Dog Writers Association of America for her work, and is currently on the board of directors of the International Association of Animal Behavior Consultants.